Love Letter to a garden

Love Letter to a Garden

by

Debbie Millman

with recipes by Roxane Gay

TIMBER PRESS
PORTLAND, OREGON

Timber Press
Workman Publishing
Hachette Book Group, Inc.
1290 Avenue of the Americas
New York, New York 10104
timberpress.com

Timber Press is an imprint of Workman Publishing, a division
of Hachette Book Group, Inc.
The Timber Press name and logo are registered
trademarks of Hachette Book Group, Inc.

Printed in China on responsibly sourced paper

Text and cover design by Debbie Millman

The publisher is not responsible for websites (or their content)
that are not owned by the publisher.

ISBN 978-1-64326-498-1

A catalog record for this book is available from
the Library of Congress.

FOR
Maria Anthis

THERE WAS NO TIME BEFORE THERE WAS TIME

The Universe began with every bit of energy contained in a very tiny incredibly dense point

It was even smaller than this point.

the point exploded with unimaginable force.

It created everything we know

and are,

and are made of

Seeds are a lot like that.

they are tiny
and densely
packed with
their entire
existence.

What does it
mean to
exist?
why are we here?
I wish I knew.

I am a Native New Yorker.
I've lived in every borough
except the Bronx. This is
me on Staten Island.

This is where my grandmother first introduced me to gardening. We were sharing an apple, and she told me if we planted the seeds, maybe a tree would grow.

We went out to our backyard and dug a hole to plant the apple seeds.

As I was digging I unearthed
a dollar bill. I was in awe.

How had it gotten there?
Did someone plant it?

I had so many questions.

It was then and there I began to associate gardening with wonder.

I became fascinated by the Yew plants in my neighborhood and collected the red berries to make my own perfume.

When my
mother
discovered they
were poisonous
she threw them
all out.

My grandparents lived in a little row house with a big backyard in Borough Park, Brooklyn. There was a chain-link fence at the far end of the yard, which opened to a shared pathway between all the houses. The trees there were huge and – as a little girl – standing beneath them made me feel like I was in a forest. I remember running as fast as I could through this deep, dark ravine until I reached the end of the path. There, I found myself facing a waterfall. Surging waves curled and fell over the edge of the alleyway and tumbled down until I couldn't see them anymore.

There was
a
waterfall
in
Brooklyn

This memory couldn't be real, and I have no idea what inspired it. Several years ago, I decided to investigate. I went to Google Maps, typed in my grandparents' address and chose the aerial satellite view. It was surreal seeing the same row of houses, the same school nearby, the same long avenues. Unsurprisingly, there was no waterfall.

But towering high above the houses were the trees, lush and verdant. They were really there!

Suddenly, I was a little girl on a little block in Brooklyn, standing beneath a canopy of towering trees as tall as the sky. As I sit with this memory, I understand how it seemed possible to a child that this forest could lead to a waterfall. Somehow.

google maps, 2008

THERE WAS NO TIME BEFORE THERE WAS TIME

My first "garden" was in a rental apartment in the West Village in 1991.

There was no grass or trees, but there was a cute little deck with pretty white brick walls. I bought lots of rose bushes and planted them with zeal in matching grey containers. There wasn't a lot of sun and I didn't know what I was doing.

Within a few weeks all the roses died.

I moved to Chelsea in 1994 and had a full-fledged back yard.

I still didn't know what I was doing.

there were two big rhododendrons already there alongside two spiky holly trees. I planted boxwood, astilbe and filled window boxes with Gerbera daisies and Moss roses. Squirrels dug up the boxes and ate the heads off the daisies. Only the boxwood and holly survived. Even the existing rhododendrons didn't make it, and I was told they were hardy. I knew some people had a green thumb, but I became convinced mine was glum.

there was an elegant bush of rather immodest white peonies that lived alongside a tangle of weeds in a rundown building on my block. I admired it nearly everyday for years and often wondered how it got there.

Who
planted it?
Did it
self-sow?

One evening, while walking home from work, I realized the peony bush was gone. There wasn't a hole where the plant had been; there wasn't any splattering of dirt or debris. Its sudden disappearance was as mysterious as its existence.

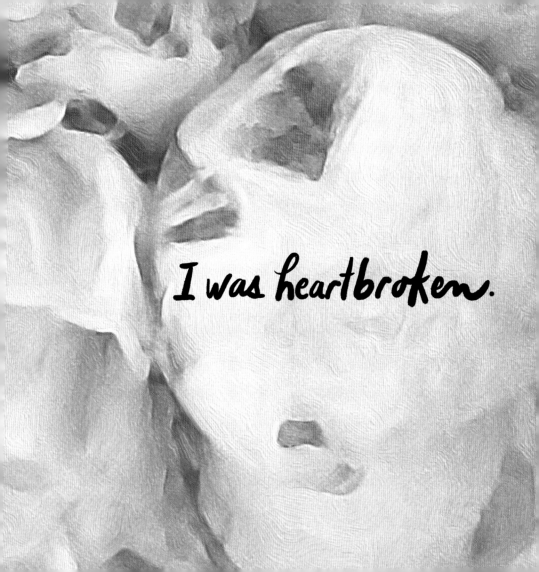

A few days later,

I ambled by the building where my beloved plant once thrived and stopped short. There was a small bouquet of white peonies in the same exact spot. I approached it slowly, gently reached out to touch the flowering buds, and realized they weren't real! Someone else mourning their absence had placed a plastic plant exactly where the real peonies had lived.

street photo, circa 2010

Real or not, my heart was a little less broken that day.

I'm always so impressed by the lengths

New Yorkers go to make their lives beautiful.

after
many years in my
apartment in Chelsea
I moved to another
apartment in
Chelsea.

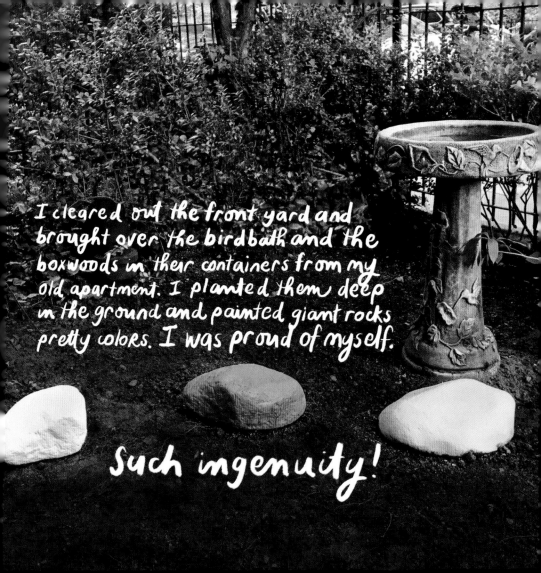

I cleared out the front yard and brought over the birdbath and the boxwoods in their containers from my old apartment. I planted them deep in the ground and painted giant rocks pretty colors. I was proud of myself.

Such ingenuity!

ALAS

The boxwoods perished as well.

I was flummoxed.
I was told that nature finds
a way. I felt I had
completely
lost mine.

I've gotten older I've become less comfortable doing anything I'm not good at. I worry I'll look ridiculous and embarrass myself. As I came face to face with the fact that I was not a good gardener, I realized it was time to ask for help. Maybe–just maybe–I could learn something new.

I began to read as much as I could about as much as I could, and to learn from some smart people around me.

This is my cousin Ilene.

She lives in Northern California and knows more about gardening than anyone I know. She took me under her wing and taught me about growing vegetables and attending to soil and how to compost. Together we planted potatoes to get more potatoes.

Which was a bit of a Revelation.

this is my friend Maria.

She was my neighbor, and a mother to me. She had a small garden outside her studio apartment filled with potted plants she tended to with care and devotion. She taught me all about city gardening.

When she passed away in 2019, I replanted her rhododendrons in my garden.

They are thriving

Days pass, hearts break,

hearts mend, days pass

Over time, my garden began to take shape.

And then everything changed.

I flew to Los Angeles to stay with my fiancée, Roxane. She suggested I pack enough underwear for two weeks.

I ended up staying for more than a year and I needed a lot more underwear.

California was beautiful But I felt unmoored.

Life was scary and uncertain.

Things We Did During COVID
(in no particular order)

1 Bought a lot of masks, plastic gloves and toilet paper

2 Set up remote offices in the house and began to work virtually

3 Learned how to play badminton

4 Worried about my friends and family incessantly

5 Watched the entire ten seasons of the television show Columbo

6 Abandoned our plans for a big wedding and eloped

7 Adopted a puppy we named Maximus Torretto Blueberry

8 Began a West Coast garden

First
some

I planted mint.

Then I got a bit ambitious.

I decided to try my hand at

Lettuces

The success buoyed me, and I began to branch out.

I grew
Radishes

Lemon
Cucumber

strawberries

The
very
first
Blue-
berry!
(aside from Max)

Twin Kirby
Cucumbers

the
teeniest
tiniest
meyer
lemon
babies

I planted corn which seemed like a longshot.

It was going well, until it wasn't and all of the corn died.

the tomatoes were easier and plentiful.

(I gave this tomato to my friend Emily.)

I also dealt with weeds

mildew and fungus

bacteria
and
bugs

and
drought.

no matter the
result, there
was nothing
like the feeling
of my hands
in the soil,

the sweetness
of the fresh
strawberries

and the pride of my first homegrown salad.

When Covid abated we began to go out again.

Being back in the world was surreal.

We returned to a very different New York, both sad and hopeful.

Our garden was messy and overgrown but mostly intact.

We even had some mushrooms.

I began
to travel
and saw
nature
in all its
splendid
diversity
up close~

The Banyan trees in Cambodia

the Woolly Moss in Iceland

Queen Victoria agave
in Mexico

Marshy lily pads in
Upstate New York

the echinacea in Singapore

the Sacred Lotus
in Japan

The Sanguine oranges in Morocco

The Pesca Regina di Londa peaches in Tuscany

The gardens in giverny and the flowers in my backyard

Despite their many differences, the flora live side by side without much rancor.

(Who knew the sweet, common daisy is considered a weed?)

there
is so
much
I learn
from
gardening:

Patience;
as I witness
the journey
from potted
plant to
planted tree,

Generosity; as I consider a mindset of abundance over scarcity.

Perspective;
as there are
so many
different
ways to see,

Alternatives; as we try to conserve water, I've learned all about succulents and the short magnificent life of their flowers.

And the
realization
that roses
really do need
a lot of sun.

As a Native New Yorker, I never imagined my childhood wonder would become a lifelong quest for a garden of my own.

I've come to realize that my garden — that any garden — is a lot like life.

Mistakes will be made,
hearts will be broken,
lessons will be learned,
love will be hoped for.

I'm so very lucky;
I get to watch things
live and grow and
fade away. When I fail,
I get to try again.

I've planted another dollar bill in another garden for another young person to discover one day.

It will be evidence that I was here.
I was here.

We are all here.

THERE WAS NO TIME BEFORE THERE WAS TIME

A note from Roxane Gay

I learned my wife Debbie enjoyed gardening a few months into our relationship, and it was something of a surprise. She was the consummate city girl, incredibly stylish, strictly adhering to her monochromatic wardrobe, walking very very fast on city streets. On a Saturday morning while I was visiting, she declared that she was going to work in the garden—a small stretch of greenery in front of what was then and is now our home in Manhattan. She got her gloves and a few tools and changed into gardening clothes and then spent hours tending to the plants, pulling weeds, turning over the soil. When she was done, she was a sweaty mess, and the garden was pristine, and she was satisfied. We spent most of the early months of the COVID-19 pandemic living together for the first time, in Los Angeles, where I lived when we met. When she saw the backyard, and a long empty planting bed, she immediately sprang into action. I ferried her to the

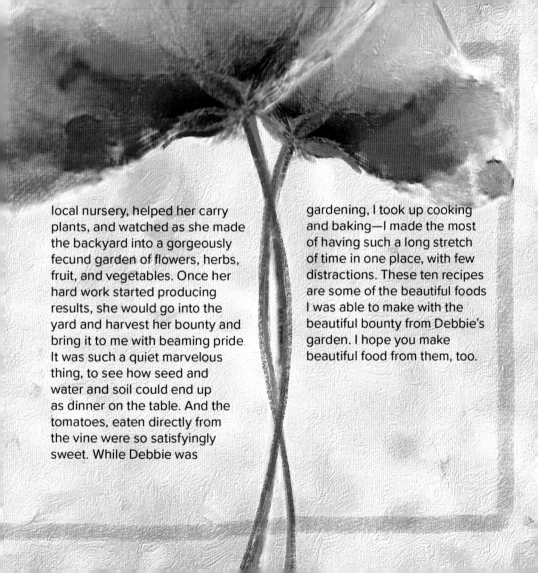

local nursery, helped her carry plants, and watched as she made the backyard into a gorgeously fecund garden of flowers, herbs, fruit, and vegetables. Once her hard work started producing results, she would go into the yard and harvest her bounty and bring it to me with beaming pride. It was such a quiet marvelous thing, to see how seed and water and soil could end up as dinner on the table. And the tomatoes, eaten directly from the vine were so satisfyingly sweet. While Debbie was

gardening, I took up cooking and baking—I made the most of having such a long stretch of time in one place, with few distractions. These ten recipes are some of the beautiful foods I was able to make with the beautiful bounty from Debbie's garden. I hope you make beautiful food from them, too.

A Summery Panzanella

CROUTONS

1 baguette, preferably
a day old

½ tsp Italian seasoning

¼ cup olive oil

DRESSING

½ cup olive oil

½ cup white
balsamic vinegar

2 tbsp Dijon mustard

2 tbsp honey

1 shallot, minced

1 clove garlic, minced

Salt & freshly cracked
black pepper

SALAD

1 bunch Italian
parsley, torn

1 bunch fresh
chives, chopped

1 bunch fresh oregano,
leaves removed
from stems

1 bunch basil, slivered

½ red onion,
thinly sliced

1 cup kalamata olives

2 pints cherry
tomatoes

8 oz fresh mozzarella,
torn into pieces

First, prepare the croutons:
Set oven to 450°. Cut the baguette in half, lengthwise, and then cut each half into thirds. Cut those thirds into 1-2 inch cubes. Season to taste with whatever spices you enjoy but a good place to start is Italian seasoning. Rub spices between your fingers to loosen up the oils then add to the croutons, Add olive oil and mix well. Place on a baking sheet and bake for 12 to 15 minutes until they reach the color and doneness you prefer. Set aside.

Then, prepare the dressing:
Whisk all the ingredients together until the dressing is well combined; adjust the ingredients as needed for desired flavor.

Finally, assemble the salad:
While you're preparing the croutons and dressings, halve the cherry tomatoes and sprinkle them with salt. When the croutons have cooled, add them to a large bowl. Add the rest of the ingredients including any liquid from the tomatoes. Once you've combined your ingredients, toss until well mixed. Add dressing. Toss until well mixed. Finish with more freshly cracked black pepper to taste. Let it sit for at least a half hour before serving so the flavors can mingle. You can substitute whatever you want. Any soft herbs will work well, including mint, dill, and the like. Feta works if you don't care for mozzarella. If you're vegan, simply omit the cheese entirely. Capers can work instead of or in addition to olives, for that extra brininess. If you really like garlic, add more garlic! Red wine vinegar works just as well as white balsamic. Ciabatta works as well as a baguette.

This is a versatile dish. While it is not, strictly speaking, a traditional panzanella, it is delicious.

A Perfect Caesar Salad

CROUTONS

1 baguette, preferably
a day old

½ tsp Italian seasoning

¼ cup olive oil

SALAD

4 heads baby gem
lettuce, chilled

2 oz (or more) fresh
Parmesan, shaved

Freshly cracked
black pepper

DRESSING

2 egg yolks

2 cloves garlic,
finely chopped

½ cup neutral oil
(vegetable, canola, etc)

4 anchovies, chopped
(anchovy paste will
also work)

½ lemon,
freshly squeezed

½ cup Parmesan
cheese, grated

1 tbsp Worcestershire
sauce

Prepare the croutons (this may look familiar):

Set oven to 450°. Cut the baguette in half, lengthwise, and then cut each half into thirds. Cut those thirds into small cubes. Season to taste with whatever spices you enjoy but a good place to start is Italian seasoning. Rub spices between your fingers to loosen up the oils then add to the croutons, add olive oil and mix well. Place on a baking sheet and bake for 12 to 15 minutes until they reach the color and doneness you prefer. Set aside.

Then, prepare the dressing:

Place two room-temperature egg yolks in a small bowl. Start whisking the eggs (you can also use a milk frother or an immersion blender or a regular blender) and slowly add a neutral oil of your choosing until the ingredients cream into a mayonnaise. Add the Worcestershire sauce and continue whisking.

Finely chop the anchovies and garlic and blend them into the dressing. Add the freshly squeezed lemon juice or more, to taste. Add salt and pepper to taste. Add ½ cup of grated Parmesan cheese. When ingredients are well combined, set aside.

Finally, assemble the salad:

Remove chilled lettuce from the refrigerator and add to a large bowl. Toss the lettuce in the dressing to taste. Less is more, here. Too much dressing will make the lettuce and croutons soggy. Add croutons and two ounces (or more) of shaved Parmesan. Dress the salad in freshly cracked black pepper because you should always bet on black. Serve.

A Tomato Galette

DOUGH

2½ cups flour

1 tbsp sugar

1 tsp salt

1 cup (227 grams) very cold butter, cubed

½ to 1 cup (or more) ice water

FILLING

3 large heirloom tomatoes

2 shallots, thinly sliced

6 oz Parmesan, gruyere or cheddar cheese, grated or shaved

1 egg

1 tbsp heavy cream

1 cup kalamata olives

2 pints cherry tomatoes, halved

8 oz fresh mozzarella, torn into pieces

First, prepare the dough:

In a mixing bowl, cut the cubes of butter into the flour until well combined. The butter should be small like little pebbles. Add sugar and salt and combine. Slowly add water until a dough forms. Recipes always lie about the amount of water this will require so start with a half cup and keep adding until all the flour has been incorporated into the dough. If it feels too wet, powder the dough with flour. Flatten into a disc, wrap in plastic, and chill for at least half an hour.

Then, prepare the galette:

While the dough is chilling, heat the oven to 400°. Thinly slice the tomatoes, and sprinkle them with salt. Let them sit. Thinly slice two shallots. When the dough is ready, cut the disc in half (there is enough dough for two galettes) and roll it out on a floured surface into a circle that is at least 14 inches in diameter.

Place a piece of parchment on a baking sheet and spray it with cooking oil. Place the galette dough on the parchment. Leaving about 2.5 inches at the edges of the dough, place the cheese (reserving 2 oz) on the dough in a circular pattern. Place the tomatoes over the cheese, in whatever way that pleases you. I find that concentric circles with the tomatoes slightly overlapping, works nicely. Then cover with the thinly sliced shallots and sprinkle with remaining cheese. Fold the edges of the crust over. Whisk the egg and cream to make the egg wash and brush it along the crust of the galette.

Bake at 400° for 35 minutes, or so. You know your oven better than I. Let cool for at least 10 minutes. It should smell great, and the galette can be served either warm or cold.

a Very Green Salad

SALAD
1 head butter lettuce
2 English cucumbers
1 bunch chives
1 bunch basil
1 bunch Italian parsley
1 bunch scallions

DRESSING
2 cloves garlic, minced
½ lemon, juiced
1 tbsp Dijon mustard
1 tbsp honey
1 shallot, minced
½ cup olive oil
½ cup red
wine vinegar
1 tsp Italian seasoning
Salt & freshly cracked
black pepper

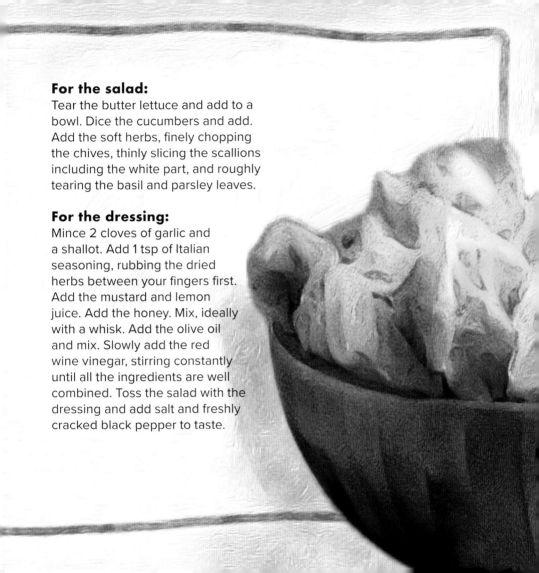

For the salad:

Tear the butter lettuce and add to a bowl. Dice the cucumbers and add. Add the soft herbs, finely chopping the chives, thinly slicing the scallions including the white part, and roughly tearing the basil and parsley leaves.

For the dressing:

Mince 2 cloves of garlic and a shallot. Add 1 tsp of Italian seasoning, rubbing the dried herbs between your fingers first. Add the mustard and lemon juice. Add the honey. Mix, ideally with a whisk. Add the olive oil and mix. Slowly add the red wine vinegar, stirring constantly until all the ingredients are well combined. Toss the salad with the dressing and add salt and freshly cracked black pepper to taste.

A MacGyver of Tomato Sauces

SAUCE

3 lbs fresh tomatoes (any combination of tomato varieties will do)

14-oz can crushed tomatoes

6 cloves garlic, thinly sliced

1 yellow onion, diced (though really, any onion will do)

3 or 4 sprigs basil

1 tbsp Italian seasoning

1 tsp oregano

½ cup olive oil

2 tbsp butter

Salt and Pepper

For the sauce:

Add the olive oil to a hot pan and then add the onion. Cook on medium high until translucent, then add the garlic and let it cook until it's just starting to brown. Add the fresh tomatoes and lower the heat. Let them cook until they've started to fall apart. Add the crushed tomatoes, fresh basil, Italian seasoning, oregano, and salt and pepper to taste. If you're feeling fancy, add a Parmesan rind.

Cover, and let simmer for at least half an hour, though the longer the sauce simmers, the better it will taste (within reason). Before removing from the heat, add the butter and stir slowly until incorporated. Let simmer for 10 more minutes.

Enjoy with most any pasta dish. It will keep in the refrigerator for at least a week.

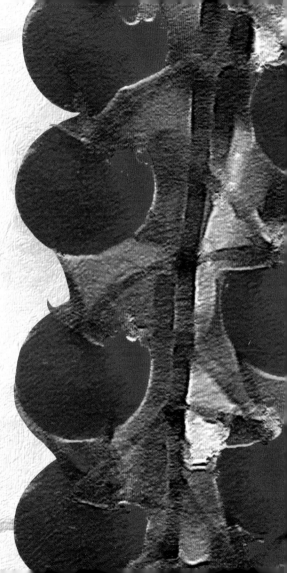

A Shaved Carrot Salad

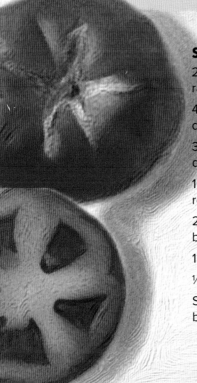

SALAD

2 large bunches rainbow carrots

4 Persian cucumbers, diced

3 Roma tomatoes, diced

1 bunch Italian parsley, roughly torn

2 cups Panko breadcrumbs

1 tbsp dried oregano

⅓ cup olive oil

Salt & freshly cracked black pepper

DRESSING

⅓ cup olive oil

⅓ cup red wine vinegar

Salt & freshly cracked black pepper

Pre-heat your oven to 425°. Combine the breadcrumbs, dried oregano, and olive oil, then spread thinly on a baking sheet. Bake for 8 to 12 minutes, until nicely browned. Set aside and let cool.

For the salad:
Peel two large bunches of rainbow carrots, then shave them. Add the shavings to a bowl along with the diced cucumbers, tomatoes, and roughly torn Italian parsley.

Prepare the dressing:
Combine the oil and vinegar, adding salt and pepper to taste. Toss the salad with the dressing. Add the breadcrumbs, to preference, which is to say, you may not want to use all of the breadcrumbs. It will be delicious, regardless.

A Mediterranean-ish Stuffed-Pita Dinner

PITAS

4 fresh pitas (naan also works)

16 oz protein of your choice (chicken, pork tenderloin, or tofu will all work nicely)

1 tsp dried oregano

½ cup olive oil

1 tbsp red wine vinegar

1 cup kalamata olives

1 lime, juiced

1 red onion, thinly sliced

8 oz white or apple cider vinegar

4 sprigs basil

8 oz fresh mozzarella, torn

16 oz cherry tomatoes, halved

2 Persian cucumbers, thinly sliced

½ cup fresh Italian parsley, torn

SAUCE

2 cups Greek yogurt

2 cloves garlic, minced

½ a lemon, juiced

1 bunch chives, finely chopped

1 tbsp red wine vinegar (white wine vinegar also works)

Season your protein with salt and pepper, to taste. In a bowl or plastic bag, combine lime juice, oregano, olive oil, and red wine vinegar. Add protein and marinate for at least an hour. When ready to cook, grill the meat, or cook it on the stovetop in a cast iron pan.

Prepare the toppings:
Thinly slice the red onion and place in a bowl. Fill the bowl with white vinegar (or apple cider vinegar) until onions are covered. Add a pinch of salt. Set aside.

Just before serving, add the prepared mozzarella, tomatoes, cucumbers, parsley, and kalamata olives to a long serving dish.

Prepare the dressing:
Add Greek yogurt to a bowl along with the garlic, lemon juice, chives, and vinegar. Mix until well combined. Add salt and pepper to taste.

Warm the pitas in the oven, at 450°, for 5 minutes. If you're feeling lazy, use the toaster or do as I do, heating them over the gas flame on the stovetop. It's fine. They just need to be warm.

To assemble:
Fill the pita first with the protein, then add desired toppings and drizzle the dressing over it all.

A Piquant Purple Cole Slaw

SLAW

1 small head purple cabbage

1 bag shredded carrots (I mean, if you want to shred your own carrots yourself feel free but science has figured this out)

½ red onion, thinly sliced

2 scallions, thinly sliced

DRESSING

1 cup mayonnaise

½ cup vinegar

1 lemon, juiced

1 tbsp Worcestershire sauce

1 tbsp honey

2 tbsp Dijon mustard

½ tsp celery seed

Salt & freshly cracked black pepper

For the slaw:
Thinly slice the cabbage and add to a bowl. If you can't find a small head of cabbage, half of a large head of cabbage will do. Add the shredded carrots, thinly sliced onion, and two scallions.

Prepare the dressing:
Add ½ cup of white balsamic vinegar and the juice of one lemon to a cup of mayonnaise. Mix well. Add the honey, mustard, and celery seed and mix well. Adjust ingredients to taste and add salt and pepper to taste.

Toss the cabbage mixture with the dressing. Chill for at least half an hour, then serve.

A Simple Fresh Tomatoes and Burrata Situation

THE SITUATION

2 large heirloom tomatoes

1 bunch basil

1 ball burrata

Good balsamic vinegar

Good olive oil

Salt & freshly cracked black pepper

To prepare:
Slice the tomatoes and arrange them as you see fit on a platter. Season the tomatoes with salt and cracked pepper. Tear the basil leaves from the stems and place over the tomatoes. Add the burrata, slightly cut open. Drizzle with olive oil and balsamic vinegar and serve.

a Strawberry Tall Cake

STRAWBERRY FILLING/TOPPING:

32 oz fresh strawberries

½ cup of sugar

WHIPPED CREAM:

2 cups heavy whipping cream

2 tbsp sugar

1 tbsp good vanilla extract

CAKE: (a modified version of Sally's Baking Addiction's vanilla cake)

1½ cups granulated sugar

3⅔ cups cake flour

1½ cups buttermilk

1½ cups GOOD butter

1 tsp salt

1 tsp baking soda

2 tsp baking powder

2 tsp good vanilla extract

3 eggs

3 egg whites

Pre-heat oven to 350°. Grease three 8-inch cake pans and line with parchment. Grease the parchment.

Halve the strawberries, place them in a bowl, and sprinkle with ½ cup of sugar so they will macerate. Set aside.

Make the cake:

If this were *The Great British Bake Off*, that's all I would say and off you would go. But for our purposes, cream the butter and sugar until it's fluffy and pale white. Add the vanilla and mix. Add the eggs, one at a time, mixing until fully incorporated and then add the egg whites. Mix. If you're fastidious, feel free to mix your dry ingredients, but the cake will still be delicious if you don't. Add 1⅔ cup of flour to the bowl, along with the salt, baking powder, and baking soda. Mix. Add ½ cup of buttermilk and mix. Add a cup of flour and mix. Add ½ cup of buttermilk and mix. Add the final cup of flour and mix. Add final ½ cup of buttermilk and mix.

Distribute the batter across the three cake pans evenly. Bake at 350° for 28 to 32 minutes.

When the cakes are ready, cool them on racks for at least 2 hours. If you're in a hurry, sure, stick them in the refrigerator or freezer. While the cakes are cooling, make your whipped cream. Add the cream, sugar, and vanilla to a mixing bowl.

Using the whisk attachment, mix at a high speed until the cream becomes whipped cream (4 minutes or so) with peaks that aren't too soft or too stiff, which is to say that they can stand but curve slightly. Don't overmix or you'll end up with butter.

When the cakes are cooled, it's time to assemble. Place the first cake layer on a cake board and spread a 1-inch layer of whipped cream across the cake. Add about ⅓ of the strawberries. Add the second layer, spread whipped cream across the cake and another ⅓ of the strawberries. Place the third cake layer atop the second layer of filling. Spread a thick layer of whipped cream across the top of the cake.

Decorate with remaining strawberries. If you're feeling fancy, you can pipe decorations with the whipped cream. Chill the cake for at least half an hour so it will set. Enjoy!

a note from Debbie Millman

The images and words in this book took six months and 60 years to create. It took six months to design, illustrate and write, and 60 years of living to bring forth the memories and experiences that comprise the stories. Almost all of the images in this book are based on photographs I've taken over the past several decades. Most of the photographs were used as reference for paintings and drawings, many were painted over, and some were used in their original format, though there are some exceptions. The flower painting on the book cover is based on a paper flower my former graduate student, Emma Herzbolzheimer, created in my branding program at the School of Visual Arts in 2021. The imagery used in A Waterfall in Brooklyn is based on a memory I brought to Midjourney to help me visualize. It took a series of prompts to arrive at something I felt was an accurate recollection, and then I used the image as reference for a water-color and a painting that I combined. Roxane Gay took the photographs of me as an adult. Otherwise, the only photographs I did not take are those of me as a child and the screen grab from Google Maps in A Waterfall in Brooklyn. These photographers remain unknown.

thank You

Eternal gratitude to Charlotte Sheedy who continues to help me grow and inspires me to share my voice.

Thank you to Makenna Goodman for inviting me to create this book and giving me the freedom to make it what it is.

For design and production help, a big thank you to Emily Weiland, Amelia Nash and Hillary Caudle.

To Elissa Altman, Glennon Doyle, Seth Godin, Mariska Hargitay, Peter Hermann, Min Jin Lee, Maria Popova and Jacqueline Woodson: thank you for your brilliance, wisdom, inspiration and kind words.

To Roxane Gay, my gratitude and infinite love for everything you are and everything you do, every day. You've helped my heart grow and flourish.

About the Authors

Named "one of the most creative people in business" by *Fast Company*, "one of the most influential designers working today" by *Graphic Design USA*, and a Woman of Influence by *Success Magazine*, Debbie Millman is also the founder of the Masters in Branding program at the School of Visual Arts, partner and editorial director of PrintMag.com, and host of the award-winning podcast *Design Matters*, one of the first and longest running podcasts in the world. She is the author of seven books, and her writing and artwork have appeared in publications including the *New York Times*, *New York Magazine*, the *Washington Post*, the *Philadelphia Inquirer*, and many more.

Roxane Gay is a widely published writer, editor, and professor who works across many genres. She is a contributing opinion writer for the *New York Times* and the editor of an eponymous imprint at Grove Atlantic. She splits her time between New York and Los Angeles and loves cooking and baking for her wife Debbie Millman.